A Pug's Guide to Happiness

Written and Illustrated by Elaine Clayton
Publisher: Lisa Hagan Books
Design: Smythtype Design

To place a wholesale or bulk order
www.lisahaganbooks.com

ISBN-13: 978-1-945962-50-9 Printed in U.S.A

A Pug's Guide to Happiness
Unleash Your Inner Pugness

By Elaine Clayton

LISA HAGAN BOOKS

Introduction

This book is a simple and easy guide to living well pug-style, with self-confidence, self-assertion and comfort. It isn't about dogma, or meditation and mindfulness. It is about the basic essentials of a life well lived: treats and sleep. And getting *your* way.

Author's Note

We pugs generally have servants who we labor
to train well, however they're not that sharp half
the time. The stress of managing them can be
detrimental to a pug's naturally imperial disposition.
This book was written with the intention to bring
wellness to every pug's mind, body and spirit and
to support each and every pug in luxurious self-
actualization. And with respect for our trainee
servants (and because charm and flattery—our most
delightful natural traits—wins the day every time) I
heretofore refer to one's "Servant" as one's "Admirer."

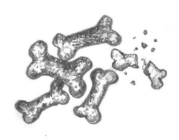

Dedicated to J.K. Veluswamy,
the best pug Admirer in the world.

signed,
Miss Georgia Sweet Tea

Gratitude

Let's start with getting out of bed in the morning.
Don't.
Don't get out of bed.

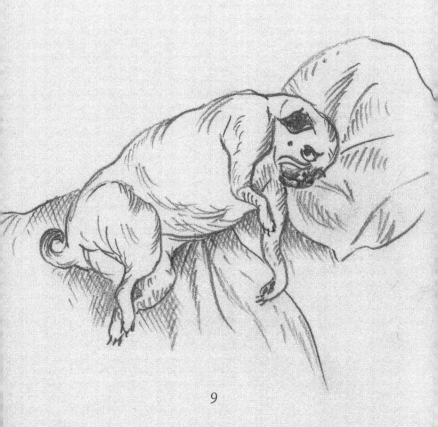

9

If you feel inspired and grateful for the olfactory property of red hot bacon crisping, this may entice you to get up, however wait until your Admirer *brings it to you in bed.*

If your Admirer fails to bring you breakfast in bed, don't be sad and remember there are other ways to acquire bacon.

Sometimes your Admirer may show aggression first thing in the morning by shoving you out of bed. *Don't even respond to this.*

15

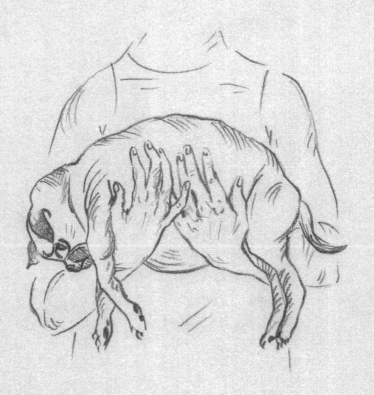

In her egotistical desire to start her dull day,
your Admirer may go to extremes.
Remain heavy.

If you are cruelly placed onto the cold floor, this is indeed painful, yet find gratitude in your ability to endure.

19

All is not lost and you know what to do
(find your comfort elsewhere)!

21

Nature:
Your Essence
is Powerful

Your first big mistake of the day may be making it all too easy for your Admirer to put the leash on, so *never, ever do that.*

Your exhilaration in the fresh morning air will bring out the fortitude in you. *Let it be known!*

Personal empowerment extends to inanimate objects as well; this speaks for itself.
Show everyone and everything who is boss.

Seeing other dogs is emotional for you, I know.
Let your emotions out always, through pulling,
barking and crying with authority (that's the only
way you know how to cry).

Yes, other dogs had the indignity to spray your hydrant, but you know you find it kind of alluring. *Go with that!*

33

Essential: Aroma therapy is excellent for your soul.

36

When you are good and ready, and only then, lead your Admirer back inside.

*Rewards:
Stop Taking
Less Than
You Deserve!*

Admirers with a hint of savvy will give you
a treat readily and immediately after the leash
is removed, which will give you unfiltered joy.

41

However, scratching on the refrigerator door
may be necessary if no biscuit is given.
*Do this repeatedly until your Admirer realizes
her disturbing misconduct.*

If that doesn't work, go straight to the cupboard where the biscuits are kept (honestly, if the Admirer is that cloddish, you've got a hard road ahead).

If that doesn't work, prepare to go air-born.
Do so with determination, your best asset!

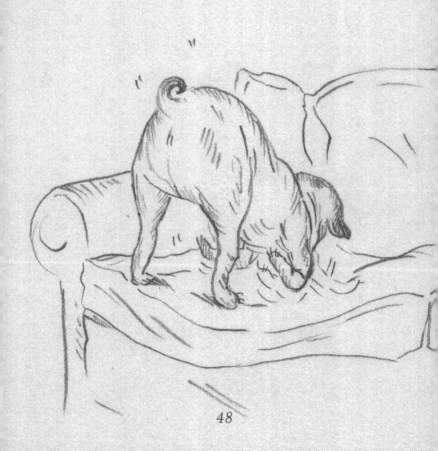

48

If your Admirer makes matters worse by giving you an undesirable biscuit, bury it because you might be okay with it later.

On a good day, your Admirer may give you a most preferred biscuit (my current favorite is cheese and liver stars)—*dash away quickly before the Admirer steals it and eats it herself!*

Alternately, (and I do hope this is rare) if
your Admirer offers you a biscuit you abhor,
be very clear in your response or *you will
suffer bad treats the rest of your days.*

Nurture:
You Are What
You Eat
So Demand
the Best

Admirers who fail to give decent treats
may also fail to produce good meals.
Stop pretending you like it, you know it is bad!

57

58

It is *en vogue* to regard scrounging
for crumbs as a diminishing practice,
however it is not beneath you. *Take the
path of least resistance and gobble it all up!*

Go commando with barking if you must, at the ghastly bowl of "kibbles" until your slap-dab Admirer *gives you some real food, even if only just slops.*

If all of these options fail to alter your Admirer's feckless caregiving, I recommend manipulation: sit a few feet away *and look as much like a sad puppy as possible (gets 'em every time!)*.

Discomfort:
Healing
the Pain

After so much discourtesy, you will need to dillydally around and try to forget about it by *picturing the world the way you want it to be.*

A patch of sunlight will miraculously transform you.

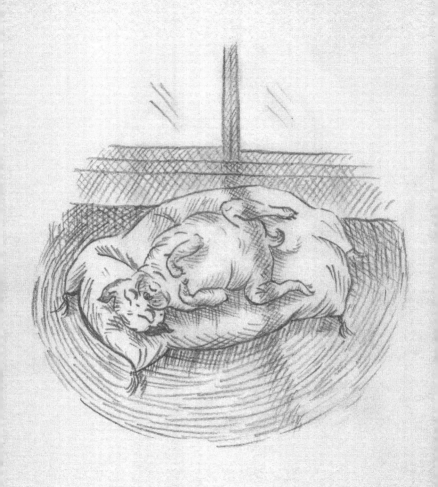

Deliveries:
Doing Good Deeds
Will Bring
You Happiness

It is a good deed to protect your Admirer
from the evil mail carrier *(unless yours is a love
and delivers you a milk bone)*.

It is a good deed to frighten sanitation
workers as they cart off last night's left overs,
insulting as that is.

If you show them who's boss, they'll tend to leave some scraps for you. Hoorah!

You are not obligated to do a good deed for the Girl Scouts unless they do the right thing (and we all know that means cookies for *you*!).

If a friend of your Admirer visits (more admirers!),
remind her of the treat she forgot to give you.
It is a good deed to allow someone else to honor you.

If you must, search for the treat yourself
and save her the trouble (but be hasty).
Lipstick tastes pretty good.

Personal Mobility:
Go In Style

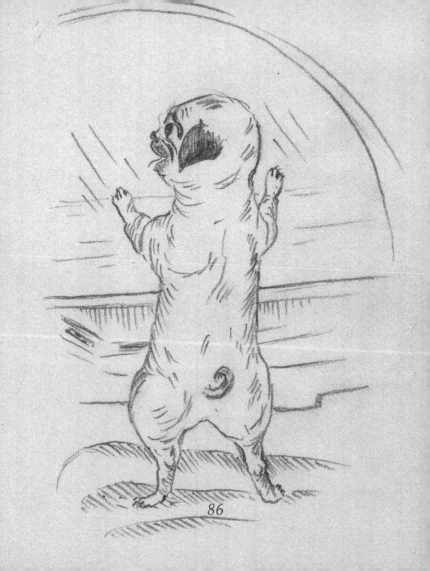

In an automobile, happiness is to urgently open any and all windows of your choice with your paw on the electronic button.

Assert your free will and natural right to sit up front, in the driver's seat.

Some pugs have been subjected to the humiliation of pet seat belts. If this is you, I can't help you much. Try prayer.

91

Road rage. It's a thing. Go with the flow.

Once you arrive at your destination,
get very cute to insure you're always
invited to come along.

95

*Holidays:
Embrace
Abundance*

You will possibly get the most luscious
food of your lifetime during holidays.

My advice is to countermand the kitchen
(no pun intended—a lot of edible action there).

Understand that you can get real food in heaps
at these times, for alas did you not know holidays
get under the Admirer's skin that way?

If your Admirer inadvertently sits at the feast table without setting a place for you, *this is war.*

Get on a child's lap.

If that fails, get on the oldest person's lap (suckers!).

Best case scenario: high chairs!
(And if all else fails try the sad puppy look again
to remind your Admirer the true meaning of
Christmas/Chanukah/Kwanza etc. etc.).

Self Care and Creative Visualization: Luxury is Your Inheritance

Don't just lay there thinking of nothing,
see it as you'd like it to be.

Personally, I envision a lilac bubbly bath.

Heated towels do wonders for a pug's self esteem.

Well, manifestly manicured is the way to go
(with another kind of bubbly)!

Loved-up and cozy, my last piece of advice
for all pugs is *never let them put you in a big bow.*
So very passé and tends to make one appear clownish.

Elizabethan collars are fine, however!
Prance and swagger, you'll be triumphant, always.

125

Also available from Elaine Clayton

Making Marks: Discover the Art of Intuitive Drawing
978-1-58270-422-7
Beyond Words/Simon and Schuster

IN SPRING 2018
A Little Bit of Angels and
A Little Bit of Fairies
from Sterling Publishers

49344608R00072

Made in the USA
Middletown, DE
13 October 2017